Kisah Hikayat Burung Gagak Hitam Dan Pembunuhan Pertama Di Bumi Edisi Bahasa Inggris

Jannah An-Nur Foundation

Published by Jannah Firdaus Mediapro Studio, 2020.

While every precaution has been taken in the preparation of this book, the publisher assumes no responsibility for errors or omissions, or for damages resulting from the use of the information contained herein.

KISAH HIKAYAT BURUNG GAGAK HITAM DAN PEMBUNUHAN PERTAMA DI BUMI EDISI BAHASA INGGRIS

First edition. December 25, 2020.

Copyright © 2020 Jannah An-Nur Foundation.

Written by Jannah An-Nur Foundation.

Table of Contents

Prolog 1

Episode 1 3

Episode 2 7

Episode 3 12

Episode 4 17

Episode 5 20

Epilog 22

Prolog

Kisah Hikayat Burung Gagak Hitam Dan Pembunuhan Pertama Di Bumi Oleh Anak Adam Edisi Bahasa Inggris Bersumberkan Dari Kitab Suci Al-Quran Serta Al-Hadist.

{Then Allah SWT sent a crow who scratched the ground to show murderer) said, 'Woe to me! Am I not even able to be as this crow and to hide the dead body of my brother?' Then he became one of those who regretted.} (The Noble Quran Surah Al-Ma'idah: 31)

Time changes everything. People's hair turns white as they grow older, but one thing always stays the same, the feathers of the crow that never change color. If anyone experienced what we, the crows, had experienced, his hair would never turn white.

As a creature I was the only eyewitness to the first crime of murder committed on the earth. I witnessed the first drop of human blood that was shed treacherously. I also knew that Allah SWT (God) was witnessing it all.

It was a very terrifying day. I knew that it was all due to Satan. How strange the actions of Satan are! How compliant human beings are to him! People love Allah SWT yet they disobey Him and while they hate Satan, they obey him. How strange the species called "humans" and how grave his contradictions are! How great Allah's mercy and forgiveness is to man! Excuse my language for I am a little bit angry.

When people experience hard times they have a saying that goes: "They were days blacker than the crow's feathers." I am aware that the crow's black color irritates people but they are oblivious to the fact that even the blackest feather on the crow's body is nothing compared to the human heart when it grows black because of sin..........

Episode 1

{*Then Allah SWT sent a crow who scratched the ground to show murderer) said, 'Woe to me! Am I not even able to be as this crow and to hide the dead body of my brother?' Then he became one of those who regretted.*} (The Noble Quran Surah Al-Ma'idah: 31)

Time changes everything. People's hair turns white as they grow older, but one thing always stays the same, the feathers of the crow that never change color. If anyone experienced what we, the crows, had experienced, his hair would never turn white.

As a creature I was the only eyewitness to the first crime of murder committed on the earth. I witnessed the first drop of human blood that was shed treacherously. I also knew that Allah SWT (God) was witnessing it all.

It was a very terrifying day. I knew that it was all due to Satan (Iblis). How strange the actions of Satan are! How compliant human beings are to him! People love Allah; yet they disobey Him and while they hate Satan, they obey him. How strange the species called "humans" and how grave his contradictions are! How great Allah's mercy and forgiveness is to man! Excuse my language for I am a little bit angry.

When people experience hard times they have a saying that goes: "They were days blacker than the crow's feathers." I am aware that the crow's black color irritates people but they are oblivious to the fact that even the blackest feather on the crow's body is nothing compared to the human heart when it grows black because of sin.

I also know that people make fun of the way a crow walks, for he hops around when he walks like a mad person walking on firebrand. He is always on the move.

So, let us assume that we walk in a strange way –hopping and leaping about. Is that not considered natural after we have witnessed the injustice inflicted by a human being upon his brother?

Before the human being was created, we used to walk about with a swinging gait like that of kings. We were proud of our black color. Then, we witnessed a brother killing his brother and from that time onward our walk has become disturbed due to the horror of the act and our children inherited our handicap.

People regard the crow's voice as being extremely ugly. It only takes for one of our species to stand on a tree and caw, for people to become pessimistic, because our caw is regarded as an evil omen.

Our voice may not be as beautiful as a nightingale's but for sure it has nothing to do with evil omen. For evil omen is a word that coincides with the actions of human beings.

A human sometimes commits a terrible act but as soon as a crow caws at the top of a tree he forgets what he has done, remembers only the crow's voice and becomes pessimistic!

It is an old trick that the human being resorts to, as there is no other creature like him to compare with how he cheats and deceives himself.

Humankind accuses crows of theft, abduction, and disobedience to their parents and families. People say that we steal kohl from eyes and soap from the rooftops of houses. But the funny thing is that we do not even know what kohl is and we do not use soap when we take baths. We do not need it because our bodies and thoughts have reached such an extent of impurity that they cannot be cleansed.

I apologize for my harsh tone but if anyone had experienced what I have experienced, he would surely have lost his mind.

I was a judge in the world of crows and a witness in the world of people. However, once a judge loses his objectivity, calmness and becomes biased, he loses his honesty and fairness. I have played both these roles together. I was a judge in the world of crows; fair, calm and neutral but when I descended to testify in the world of humans, I lost my competence as a judge and my calmness and I screamed. Then Allah sent me to teach the son of Adam a lesson in mercy.

That day, long ago I said to Cain (Qabil) while I was cawing reproachfully in my sharp voice, "We know that you are a brutal murderer and in spite of that you are ignorant; in spite of the fact that you are a human being assumed to be knowledgeable. An ignorant person who is oblivious of being ignorant; an ignorant person who does not know how to bury his brother's body."

I apologize for I am still quite worked up.

Sometimes I think of what happened calmly and objectively like a judge. It is true that aggression is a characteristic of all creatures. Sometimes a crow is aggressive against the group and when that happens, a trial is assembled.

It is known that crows have courts that abide by the laws of justice. These trials take place when a certain crow steals another crows' nest, another crows' female or the food of young crows.

Each crime has its own penalty. When a crow steals another's nest we tear down the stolen nest, severely censure the violator and make him build another nest for that crow. In the case of stealing another crow's female, the group kills the crow in question with their beaks. When a crow steals the food of young crows, the group pulls out that crow's feathers until he becomes just like the young crows that are without feathers.

Sometimes in addition to censure and pulling out feathers another penalty is added, which is banishment from the group.

In fact the trials of crows are usually held in an open space or in a wide field. Those who precede others in attendance have to wait for the rest of the group.

So, we wait for days and nights till our number is complete. Then, we appoint someone to guard the violator and the trial begins.

The whole group starts cawing together. The accused one caws back. In their turn, the witnesses caw and flap their wings in rage and anger.

Episode 2

The accused crow caws and flaps his wings in return.

Then finally, the accused lowers his wings, ducks his head and stops cawing. This is taken as his confession to the crime.

At this stage, the judge pronounces his sentence and all the crows flock upon the guilty one tearing him to death with their beaks. After that, the crows caw successively and flyaway.

One of them will then carry away the crow's dead body to be buried.

The dead crow may be guilty but death has a sanctity that obligates honoring the body by burying it.

In this way crows implement justice in two cases -life and death. This is because justice is the strongest instinct that crows, have. Originally, justice in the world of humans is acquired and remains relative, but in the world of crows, it is instinctive and absolute.

There are some essential rules of ours that are not subject to change or substitution and whoever goes against them goes against the group and thus deserves to be despised and killed.

These rules and laws have not been established by crows. They have been bestowed upon us by Allah SWT. Who made them a part of our innate nature and a duty to be abided by. We do not constitute laws for ourselves.

We know that the soul is inclined to follow its desires and is Partial to whatever is in its interest. Since crows have surrendered to the legislation of the Creator, they have reached the shore of safety. In fact, working in the field of law requires a person to separate himself from his desires, and no creature can do so except for the angels.

Mentioning angels reminds me of the first days of creation. The earth was so peaceful before the human being descended upon it.

No ship had exploited the pure sea, the wind was so pure as it had not touched the forehead of a human being and all the fields on this earth had never been trod on by humans. The life was still pure and not contaminated by even one single lie. Everything was pulsating with sincerity.

The mountains were covered with white snow that shone under the rays of the setting sun. The seas' blue chest heaved up and down as it sighed and the air was intoxicated from the perfume of green fields. Even though everything was exquisitely beautiful and enchanting, there was something missing from the scene ...

This missing element was that the human being should submit himself humbly to Allah SWT and supplicate. Only then the real meaning behind this abstract beauty would surface. Things acquire less beauty and more meaning once they have knowledge, commit a mistake and then beg for mercy.

This is how it always has been with knowledge. Innocence is grazed in the beginning, and then knowledge is the result. Allah's angels are endowed with innocence. As for humans, their innocence was grazed in paradise. It was stolen by the devil for a certain eternal divine wisdom, which is, inhabiting and populating the earth. We knew that the human had come from paradise.

In the beginning it was tears, as Adam and Eve's crying on the earth was an extremely moving scene. We knew then from the sound of those tears the enormity of guilt, the meaning of disobedience and the Sincerity of repentance.

Adam aimed at nothing but to achieve repentance. How great was his dignified face! In his eyes, there was a limitless tenderness of a father that does not favor one child to another.

As for Eve (Hawa), she was the mother of all the women on this earth.

They both supplicated to Allah SWT saying, "Our Lord! We have wronged ourselves. If You forgive us not, and bestow not upon us Your Mercy, we shall certainly be of the losers."

Eve bore her first child. Humans do not lay eggs like us birds, but they bear children.

In each pregnancy Eve bore a boy and a girl at the same time. The boy of the first pregnancy could lawfully marry the girl of the second pregnancy and vice versa. Eve gave birth to Gain—and his sister Aklima and Abel (Habil) and his sister Liyotha and their siblings grew up together.

Abel came running down the hill laughing, his face clearly pronouncing all his eight years of age and in pursuit came Cain holding in his hand a tree branch -trying to catch up with his brother. They were playing together as usual.

I do not know why one brother was as gentle as a field lily and the other as harsh as a mountain thorn. It always happened that Cain would choose to play the role of the hunter and give Abel the role of the prey. When the playing heated up Cain's eyes would shine with hate as he showered Abel with strokes from the tree branch in his hand.

In the beginning Abel would laugh, his laugh would vibrate between the hills and trees, like a book illuminated with purity and happiness. Then Cain would hold the tree branch harshly with his two hands instead of one, so the strokes would be more painful. At that point, pain instead of happiness would be drawn all over Abel's face and the sound of his laugh would turn into something like a scream.

Then Prophet Adam AS would come running to them and find Abel wounded and Cain would still be continuing his attack. Adam would scream saying, "Cain! What have you done to your brother?" Then Cain would reply, "We are playing and Abel has chosen to be the prey."

After that, Adam would scream, scolding Cain and then separate the two brothers. He would scold Cain and wipe the wounds of his kind son. He would talk to them telling them that they were brothers from the same mother, and that they lived on the same earth. For that reason they should join together in love, not hate.

What surprised me was that Cain would shut his harsh mouth without defending himself, while on the other hand Abel would defend his brother begging his father to forgive them both.

Episode 3

Time passed and they turned twenty. At that time Cain raised his hand and slapped Abel's face and screamed, "This is my hut." He left red fingerprints on his brother's face. Abel was surprised by the insult. Anger swelled up inside him and fast tortured tears collected in his eyes.

Abel said innocently, "Look at my hands! They have become raw from building the hut."

Cain then replied with determination, "You will not spend the night in the hut after today's sunset. Cain has spoken his words. "

After that Abel tenderly replied, "I too want to have my say in this. I love you Cain so why are you doing this?"

However, Cain heard nothing as he had left the place.

I did not see Abel telling Adam about what happened. I do not know why, maybe he felt that his father's heart was full of sadness from the things Cain had done and he was afraid that he would only deepen that sadness. Or he may have said to himself that Cain's threats were only words that would not be carried out. When the time of sunset arrived, Abel was surprised by his brother barging into his hut and in his hand there was a sharp edged rock. Before Abel could even open his mouth the rock cracked his forehead and blood came pouring out. Then Cain carried him and threw him out of the hut. Abel bandaged his wounds with herbs and went to sleep in his place. After that, Adam was surprised to find his son sleeping outside of his hut and that there was dry blood on his forehead. Adam screamed his usual scream, only this time it stemmed from a deeper sadness, "Cain! What have you done to your brother Abel?"

Cain did not look like Abel and neither did Aklima look like Lyotha. Cain was crueler than Abel and Lyotha was not as pretty as Aklima. Abel was supposed to marry Aklima and Cain was supposed to marry Lyotha. Personally, I favored Abel to his brother and I was content that he would be marrying the prettier of the two. Abel does not get angry when we eat from his food. One day Abel saw me standing in front of the chicken eggs he was raising, so he put out his hand and gave me an egg and I was so happy for his cooperation with our kind. This man was aware of the wisdom behind cooperation between creatures and was aware of the meaning of mercy. He was a man who knows, loves and fears Allah.

I want to concentrate, so I can testify to all the destruction and ruin, and tell it to the wind that whistles in the most desolate places.

Cain screamed, "No, I am better than him!" The devil was behind his words. Satan said the same about Adam, and that day he taught it to Adam's son, so he could say it about his brother.

Cain again screamed in front of his father, "I will not marry Lyotha. I will marry Aklima! We were together in the same womb. I am more entitled to her!"

Adam explained to his son that it is unlawful to marry his sister. Cain refused to change his stance. I was surprised at his boldness and I did not know how Adam would react to this.

Then Adam said, "May each of you offer a sacrifice to Allah, and whoever's sacrifice is accepted is right."

Adam withdrew from trying to judge between them and left that to heaven.

I did not know how Allah would accept their sacrifices. I did not even know what was meant by sacrifice.

I waited for a few days in which I was busy solving problems in the world of the crows. At that time, there was a fugitive crow we were looking for to put to trial.

Then came the day of offering sacrifices to Allah. Abel came carrying one of his largest rams and he left it on the mountain and prayed to Allah to accept it. Cain came and with him he brought ears of wheat that had not yet ripened. As Cain was stingy to the extent that we crows could not even taste his food, Cain offered his sacrifice and walked away.

The two brothers stood back.

In my heart, as I am an unbiased judge, I wished that Allah would accept Abel's sacrifice. Down came a fire from the sky that devoured Abel's sacrifice as a sign of acceptance. Abel shouted for joy and Cain screamed, "Murder!"

Cain stood with his palms extended in front of him gazing with his eyes into the horizon. Despite his silence, there was a wave of enmity vibrating from him that was almost tangible.

It was a wonderful day. The sun was spreading its warmth into the atmosphere and the pine trees that lined the horizon were bathing in the rays of the sun. Its branches took the color of amber that comes from the seas. From the nearby mountains blew a wind that carried with it from the depths of the coral reef that is covered with the forests green velvet, the perfume of the virgin forest and gorgeous flowers.

Then once again Cain screamed, "I will kill you."

Abel did not know why Cain was so angry with him. Indeed, purity usually does not know the motives of evil. Allah had accepted from one and refused the other.

Abel told his brother that Allah accepts only from the pious. Again, Cain murmured, "I will kill you."

Abel replied, as he was turning around to go back to his hut, *"If you do stretch your hand against me to kill me, I shall never stretch my hand against you to kill you, for I fear Allah; the Lord of the 'Alamin (mankind, Jinn, and all that exists). Verily, I intend to let you draw my sin on yourself as well as yours, then you will be one of the dwellers of the Fire, and that is the recompense of the Zhalimun (polytheists and wrong doers)."*

Abel walked away with his wife Aklima. They got married and when the signs of pregnancy started to appear on her, Cain decided to kill his brother.

We were able to find the guilty crow that had escaped and so his trial began.

Episode 4

Abel laid down on the ground after a day of hard work. He went to sleep as soon as he laid his head upon a bed of lilies. The sun made its way towards the west.

The trial of the sinning crow continued.

Sunset befell the sky and Cain came and in his hand was a donkey's jaw that he had found in the forest.

A donkey had died in the nearby forest and beasts of brey had eaten his meat and the vultures had eaten what was left of him and the earth had drunk his blood and only his bony jaw was left on the ground.

Cain carried the first weapon used on earth and started to look for his brother. He found him sleeping, so he moved towards him.

Something which I could not understand in the noble dreaming face moved him.

Abel then woke up and opened his eyes. Cain raised his hand and struck down with the bony jaw. Blood spluttered from Abel's face onto Cain's chest. The sinning hand struck the kind face once again. On the fifth strike Cain's hand hit the mud of the field.

Abel laid completely motionless and Cain then realized that his brother had died. His hand ceased striking its fast and vicious strikes and he sat frowning in front of his victim.

We still have not finished with the trial of the sinning crow as we postponed the trial until the next day and appointed someone to guard the crow and then we left.

I stood at the top of a tree above Cain's head and cawed screaming, "Cain! What have you done to your brother Abel?"

Cain raised his head and looked at me. His body was trembling.

The trial of the accused crow took hours. He was lying. He denied the accusations ascribed to him, but as the trial advanced, the noose around his neck was tightening. All the time the trial was proceeding, Cain was walking and carrying his brother on his back.

He did not know what to do with his corpse. Vultures were circling above it and wild animals were lured by its smell. Cain was afraid that the wild animals would devour his brother if he left him, so he walked along carrying him on his back.

He did not know what to do with him or how to act.

The crow's trial was over and all the accusations ascribed to him were proven. The judges sentenced him to death. The sinning crow's sentence was executed. I carried the dead crow to bury him in a far away place. While I was flying, I felt an unseen force guiding my wings towards Cain. I had no intention of passing by Cain, as I did not like him, but my wings, despite my will, were heading towards him. Something exalted that surpassed my perception was guiding my wings.

Episode 5

One of the honored angels ordered me, "O crow! Allah (Blessed and Exalted be He) is sending you to show the son of Adam how to bury his brother's body."

Upon that, I instantly landed with my burden in front of Cain. Then I put the dead crow in front of me and started digging in the ground. I dug the ground with my claws and beak. After that, I arranged the dead crow's wings against his body and pushed him with my beak into his grave. I screamed two short screams, and then covered him with sand.

After that, I looked at the son of Adam. My look clearly said this, "Even though we justifiably killed him we still owe his body the right to be respected. But you ..."

After that, I started cawing in his face and then finally I took flight towards the west.

As I was flying away, I heard Cain's scream, "O woe to me. I have failed to be like this crow and bury my brother's body."

I imagined that his scream was burning with remorse. I did not know from which spring his remorse flowed. Was he remorseful because he had been carrying him around all this time without knowing that he had to bury him? Or was he remorseful because he had unjustifiably killed him? I do not know. All I wanted to know was the condition of Abel's wife. I felt tranquility when I knew that she was about to give birth. I wanted to be reassured that the human race came from the lineage of a strong generous man who feared Allah. I know that the children of Cain, the first murderer, would fill the earth. I know that the conflict between them and the children of the kind martyr Abel would never stop. Maybe even the father's tragedy would be repeated with the children.

All this I know but I am ignorant of the wisdom behind that. It is not my business to know. I was a witness to the son of Adam and a teacher to him for a period of time but it is not my job to know why.

Maybe the human knows.....

Epilog

Narrated 'Abdullah:

The Prophet said, "No human being is killed unjustly, but a part of responsibility for the crime is laid on the first son of Adam who invented the tradition of killing (murdering) on the earth. (It is said that he was Qabil). (Sahih Hadith)

'Uthman bin 'Affan narrated that the Prophet Muhammad SAW said:

"There is no right for the son of Adam in other than these things: A house which he lives in, a garment which covers his nakedness, and Jilf (a piece of bread) and water." (Sahih Hadith)

Narrated Anas:

The Prophet said, "Allah SWT will say to that person of the (Hell) Fire who will receive the least punishment, 'If you had everything on the earth, would you give it as a ransom to free yourself (i.e. save yourself from this Fire)?' He will say, 'Yes.' Then Allah SWT will say, 'While you were in the backbone of Adam, I asked you much less than this, i.e. not to worship others besides Me, but you insisted on worshipping others besides me.' (Sahih Hadith)

Narrated Abu Huraira:

Prophet Muhammad SAW said, "Allah SWT (God) created Prophet Adam AS in His picture, sixty cubits (about 30 meters) in height. When He created him, He said (to him), "Go and greet that group of angels sitting there, and listen what they will say in reply to you, for that will be your greeting and the greeting of your offspring."

Adam (went and) said, 'As-Salamu alaikum (Peace be upon you).' They replied, 'AsSalamu-'Alaika wa Rahmatullah (Peace and Allah's Mercy be on you) So they increased 'Wa Rahmatullah' The Prophet added 'So whoever will enter Paradise, will be of the shape and picture of Adam Since then the creation of Adam's (offspring) (i.e. stature of human beings is being diminished continuously) to the present time." (Sahih Hadith)

It was narrated that Shaddad bin Aws said:

"The Last Messenger of Allah SWT (God) said: 'The best of your days is Friday. On it Adam was created, on it the Trumpet will be blown, on it all creatures will swoon. So send a great deal of peace and blessings upon me on that day, for your peace and blessings will be presented to me.' A man said: 'O Messenger of Allah, how will our peace and blessings be shown to you when you will have disintegrated?' He said: 'Allah SWT has forbidden the earth to consume the bodies of the Prophets.'" (Sahih Hadith)